Garden Photo Shoot

A Photographer's Yearbook of Garden Wildlife

To Margaret
With best wishes from John

John Thurlbourn

J Thurlbourn

Brambleby Books

Garden Photo Shoot: A Photographer's Yearbook of Garden Wildlife
© John Thurlbourn 2009

ISBN 978-0-9553928-3-2

Published 2009 by
BRAMBLEBY BOOKS
Luton, Bedfordshire, UK
www.bramblebybooks.co.uk

Cover design and book layout by Creatix Design Services
Cover photos by John Thurlbourn

Printed on FSC paper by
Cambrian Printers, Aberystwyth, UK.

Garden Photo Shoot

ACKNOWLEDGEMENTS

Firstly, my thanks to Nicola and Hugh Loxdale from Brambleby Books for all their help, for without them there would be no book, and Tanya Warren, Creatix, for all the work she has put into the lovely design of my book. Thanks to Peter Dell for his Foreword and to my partner Jill Tripp for her support and taking my portrait photo in the book. I also thank Peter Harvey for his help in identifying the spiders, David Robinson and Judith Marshall for identifying the crickets and grasshoppers, Henry Curry for help in identifying the dragon- and damselflies, Fritz Geller-Grimm for identifying the Empidid fly and Bill Symondson for help in identifying the slugs and snails.

DEDICATION

I dedicate this book to my grandchildren Harry and Charlotte Stoten. I hope that it will encourage them to love and enjoy the wildlife around them and help in any way they can to preserve it. With the loss of habitat and climate change all wildlife is having a hard time – from birds and animals to insects and plants. All this affects our lives and we need to preserve them for the sake of the planet.

Contents

11   About the Author

13   Foreword

14   Introduction

16   Birds

44   Mammals

56   Butterflies and moths

64   More insects and spiders

88   Frogs, snakes, slugs and snails

94   Bibliography and Useful Websites

95   Biodiversity in my garden

About the Author

About 20 years ago, John Thurlbourn became interested in photography. His first camera was a manual SLR camera and he had his own darkroom. He took mainly black and white photographs of sporting activities and portraits.

His other interests were animals and wildlife generally, which he preferred to photograph in colour using colour transparency film. The cost of producing colour prints from these proved to be very high and restricted him in the numbers he could afford to do. Nevertheless, it was a hobby he loved, and he was taking more and more photographs and trying new challenges. With the then costs of film, paper and chemicals, he had to make every shot count, which limited him from trying new techniques and experimenting with exposures and shutter speeds.

However, when digital photography came along it opened up a whole new world for him. He started with a 3 megapixel camera, using a 10x optical zoom lens. This brought the fun back into photography, and he was able to take hundreds of photographs and try all sorts of techniques to get the effects he wanted without having to worry about the costs.

For twelve years he had been a manager of a hardware shop; previous to that he was a postman. It was as a postman that he actually developed the love for photography. John had always had pets like dogs, cats, rabbits and birds and had helped his wife looking after her horse. In 1998, he started work at the Royal Veterinary College, North Mymms, Hertfordshire, caring for the animals which he found enjoyable. He loved looking after them from the very first day.

John Thurlbourn

Foreword

I feel very fortunate to have met and bonded with John thirty years ago. He was a budding photographer and as I was a humble snapper of pictures, but had a keen interest, we struck up a friendship that has lasted to this day.

The inherent pleasure of taking a quality photograph was instilled in me, as my wife and I went on numerous trips, birdwatching, and country rambles with John. We watched and listened, as John seemed to photograph and explain about each wild thing we came across, whether it was animal, bird, insect or plant.

His knowledge and real love of nature and wildlife is plain to see in the production of this charming book.

Such inspiration is the result of hard work and I for one would like to state that John is a true naturalist, but above all, he is a true and much loved friend.

Peter Dell
August 2008

Introduction

In April 2001, I moved into one of the cottages in Hawkshead Lane, North Mymms, Hertfordshire. The first thing I noticed was the lack of bird life in the garden; in actual fact there was none. The previous tenant had two large aviaries with 12 species of foreign birds and so the native birds stayed away. After clearing all traces of the aviaries and bird droppings, I put up several feeders around the patio. It took about a month before any birds were visiting the garden on a daily basis. By the summer of 2006, I had had 41 species of bird come to the garden and of those there were 18 species that visited the garden daily all year round.

It was in early 2004 that I first noticed signs of foxes coming to the garden and it was through setting up a light and watching them that I thought of photographing every living creature in my garden. As I built up a portfolio of the wildlife I thought it would be good to put all the photos and information into a book.

It was amazing how much there was to see and photograph in the garden. I did not realise just how many moths, butterflies, bees, beetles, flies, and spiders as well as birds, foxes and other animals there were. It is fascinating to watch the birds and foxes going about their daily lives and how they struggle to survive and knowing that I help in a small way to make their lives a little easier. Judging by the number of young birds of all kinds there are in the garden, the population here is thriving and that's another reason to feed them, not just in winter but all year round. House Sparrows and finches are not in decline around here.

I never get bored seeing the foxes; they visit at all times and I am disappointed when they come to the garden in the early hours and I miss them. They visit at different times of the day and night; since this is how nature works. If they came at the same time each day they would be vulnerable to their predators (mainly man) and their prey would know when they were coming, so would avoid the area, although in the case of my garden, the eggs and peanuts I put out for them are unlikely to go anywhere. It's also fascinating watching the butterflies, moths and all the other insects going about their busy lives, surviving just to produce the next generation and in the process, helping the plant life.

Friends who have read the manuscript, have said how much they enjoyed it; they also liked the photographs. They said I should do something with it, so I decided to try and get it published. I hope the book will encourage others to go out into their gardens and discover the wonderful world of wildlife on their doorsteps. Maybe the photographs in it will encourage them to have a go at photography as well.

Photography is such a great pastime and the digital camera has made it possible for everyone to try. You don't even have to have the photos printed if you do not want to as you can plug the camera into your TV and have a slide show. It's a great way for you to share your photos with family and friends.

You don't have to know what the names of the creatures are or all about their lifestyle to appreciate wildlife. I take photographs just for the sheer enjoyment I get from photography. I'm self-taught and learn by making mistakes (not costly with digital) and I think it's a good fun way to learn. I love everything to do with photography – from the taking and printing of photos to looking at them, whether in print or as slide shows. I also love to see other peoples' photographs because you see a bit of that person in them. Just as painters express themselves in their paintings, each person puts a bit of themselves into their photos and you learn a little about them and their lives.

It's a wonderful natural world on your doorstep – if you just take the trouble to go out and look for it. Once you do you will lose yourself in it and find it very therapeutic. I'm sure you will come to love it just as I do and spend many happy hours studying nature at work.

Leisure
W.H. Davies (1911)

What is this life if, full of care,
We have no time to stand and stare.

No time to stand beneath the boughs
And stare as long as sheep and cows.

No time to see, when woods we pass,
Where squirrels hide their nuts in grass.

No time to see, in broad daylight,
Streams full of stars, like skies at night.

No time to turn at Beauty's glance,
And watch her feet, how they can dance.

No time to wait till her mouth can
Enrich that smile her eyes began.

A poor life this if, full of care,
We have no time to stand and stare.

Birds

Many kinds of birds visit my garden and often in good numbers. For example, I have had as many as 11 **Blackbirds** in the garden at one time. Their favourite food includes pieces of apple that I put out for them. It is good to watch them in the spring, gathering the moss from my lawn for their nests. I also love to watch them bathing in the little pools on the waterfall of my pond. I have yet to see them bathe in the bird bath. Many of the bird photographs that you see below were taken from my bedroom window. This gives a nice, natural look to the background.

The **Long-tailed Tits** visit my garden in late November; they usually come in the early morning and about an hour before sunset. I get flocks of up to a dozen birds. They feed on the

Long-tailed Tit

fat balls and their favourite peanut feeder; however, I have never seen them on the sunflower feeder. They stay until the end of April and then I don't see them again until late November.

One day in March, about a year after I had moved in, I looked out of my bedroom window and saw something on my pond. It was a while before I realised that it was a pair of **Mallard** ducks (p.18). They stayed for about three weeks, then disappeared. I thought that would be the last I saw of them, but no, they have since returned every year in late February or early March and

Left to right: Juvenile, male and female Blackbird

A pair of Mallard ducks

Song Thrush

Pied Wagtail

stayed around for a couple of weeks or so, before flying off until the following year. I look forward to seeing them as I feel winter is almost over when they arrive.

The Mallards waddle down the garden to the flower bed, have a feed on the sunflower hearts, fruit and peanuts and then waddle back to the pond as though they own the place.

I thought I stood a fair chance of photographing most of the bird species that visited the garden but didn't hold out much hope of seeing, let alone photographing, a **Goldcrest**. A single bird was spotted by a friend one June evening the same year, and I got a glimpse of it before it disappeared and have not seen it again since.

The **Song Thrush** is another lovely song bird that sadly has only visited my garden but once. It was a very cold February day in 2003, and I managed to get this photograph of it before it went on its way.

On the same day I photographed a pair of **Pied Wagtails** which regularly came to my patio. They did a lovely job of clearing up all the food that the other birds dropped on the ground. They are one of the most difficult birds to photograph as they are constantly on the go.

I was not having any luck attracting **Gold-finches** into my garden, yet there were quite

Feeding time for a
family of Goldfinches

Goldfinch

a few at the front of the house. When in March 2003 I changed from feeding black sunflower seeds to sunflower hearts, I saw within a couple of weeks to my delight a pair of Goldfinches feeding on the seeds.

One year on, I had as many as eight visiting the feeders. It was good watching them along with the Greenfinches jostling for a perch.

Chaffinches (p.20) are another species that visit in large numbers. They are very busy birds, scampering about, mainly getting scraps that other birds leave behind. They are rarely seen to feed from the seed feeders but prefer the flower bed or feed on the patio below the fat ball or peanut feeders and also got used to my new bird

Dunnock

table which was presented to me by my friends at the veterinary college on my 60th birthday in 2004.

The **Dunnock** is another busy little bird, darting around and feeding from the ground. I never saw this species on any of the feeders and very rarely on the bird table, probably because they feed mainly on insects and seed scraps. I think the male has one of the nicest little songs heard in the garden; you have to be quiet as it is very soft, not loud for all to hear, as in the case of the Wren.

They say that the **House Sparrow** is in decline, but I am pleased to say it is not the case in my garden. I had large numbers of them visiting; as many as a dozen birds could be seen at any one time. They are quite dominant and saw off any other bird which tried to get on the feeder when they were there. It was good to see them bathing, as often there were two or three at a time.

Chaffinch

Chaffinch nest with young

House Sparrows: female left and male right

Some were juveniles which just stood on the edge being showered by the others.

Greenfinches can be quite aggressive towards other birds on the sunflower heart feeder. They hover like a humming bird and peck until the other bird or birds have gone away so that they can perch and feed. This happened especially with Goldfinches, as I noticed that they also tend to stand on the perch and eat the seeds.

A **Grey Heron** (p.22) turns up from time to time. Quite often it lands on top of my shed before moving down to the pond. I had prepared a trip wire going all the way round the pond. This consisted of plastic-coated wire pegs, about a foot high, with three strands of

Magpie snatching a nut

Grey Heron

Cock Pheasant

Magpie

thick nylon line threaded through them, about nine inches from the water's edge. I would not go so far as to say that it was a one hundred percent sure way to stop the heron getting the fish, but this measure was very successful over the last three years. The main thing was that it did not harm the bird. They are beautiful birds for sure and have a hard time, especially in harsh winters when food is difficult to come by. This is the only photo that was not taken in my garden; it was actually taken at Gobions Lake, Hertfordshire. I really like it, as the bird has been captured in flight and the early morning sunlight adds to the mood of the picture.

A cock **Pheasant** started visiting my garden in March 2004, three years after I moved in. Prior to this, I was very puzzled as to what was crushing my daffodils, until one day I saw him. He was as happy as Larry, lying on my flower bed. I could not be upset, as he is such a magnificent creature in his full breeding plumage.

A couple of **Magpies** regularly come into the garden. They mostly feed on the bits of the fat balls that have fallen to the ground, then have a drink from the bird bath and bathe in the waterfall. I feel a bit sorry for the Magpie as it gets a 'bad press', many saying that they eat young birds and eggs; this is true, but only in a very few cases. Their main diet is insects, fruit and animal road kills. Let's face it: cars and cats kill a thousand times more than the Magpie does. Thus, the Magpie is a welcome visitor to my garden.

Starling youngster

Starling in winter plumage in early spring with female sparrow behind

23

Starling squabbles

Starlings on my lawn...

...and at the bath

Juvenile Starling

I love **Starlings**; they are such characters. They use so much energy when they bathe that the water goes everywhere and I always have to replenish it when they have finished. I have yet to see them bathe in the waterfall though.

It's only when you take the time and get a good look at the Starling that you realise what a very striking and beautiful bird it is (p.23). As with the Sparrow, we tend to just think "Oh, it's only a Starling or Sparrow", but they have such lovely markings and they are so full of life.

Juvenile Starlings cause quite a din with their constant squabbling, but I can't help liking them. I counted up to 43 on my lawn at one time in July. On page 23, a youngster tries to get some of their favourite food, lard balls. At this time of year, they get through five or six large ones a week.

A flock of Starlings in the field at the bottom of the garden

Bath time

25

Jay stealing nuts

In early April 2004, I started putting peanuts out for the Pheasant and within five minutes a pair of **Jays** came down. They became regular visitors throughout the day but are timid birds. They first landed in some shrubs, as in the second photo, to take a good look round and to see if the coast was clear, before moving onto the ground to feed on the peanuts.

One day in the same month of April I saw and photographed what I thought to be a Coal Tit. When I looked at the photo, I noticed it did not have a white stripe on the black hood at the back of its neck. I looked it up in one of my bird books and, to my surprise, found that it was in fact a **Marsh Tit**.

I had never seen the species before so was doubly delighted to have seen a single bird in my garden and managed to get photographs of it as well. It was a regular visitor for about four or five weeks thereafter, and I hoped this was not the last I had seen of it.

Jay, a wary watcher

Marsh Tit

Wood Pigeon

On the 1st of May, I was standing by my pond looking at the fish. Behind me I could hear this lovely bird song. I looked round and saw a cock **Linnet**, singing his heart out. I got my camera and managed to take a few photos. He just stayed there without a care in the world. I had never seen a Linnet in this area before and he has not alas returned. I hope he does, as his is such a lovely sound to hear in the garden.

This male **Wood Pigeon** seemed to spend most of his day in my garden or in the tree above the pond. I had only seen him, never any other. I did feel sorry for him as he seemed

Little Owl

to be 'Billy no mates'. I know some people don't like Wood Pigeons which they regard as vermin. He was a very good-looking specimen and was not doing any harm. I am pleased to say that as of September 2004, other Wood Pigeons have joined 'Billy no mates'. There were as many as five at one time.

I have seen a **Little Owl** on five or six occasions. As yet I have not been able to photograph it as it sits in the maple tree at the bottom of the garden at about sun set. So flash photography was out of the question. All I could do was hope that it would come earlier some day. I saw and heard Little Owls very often over the road in the caravan field and also in the park field when I was at work (above). I was able to get the photograph (left) of a youngster taking refuge in a hole at the base of an oak tree in the park field, close to my house.

Carrion Crows

Carrion Crows started visiting the garden in early May 2004. They made short work of the peanuts left by the foxes. These birds are very difficult to photograph since at the slightest movement they are off. I managed to get a photograph early one morning from my bedroom window. The Crow was too busy drinking to notice me. In the next few years, they started coming in groups of three or four, so were clearly becoming a little less timid.

In the evening of the 30th May, I saw a bird on my greenhouse roof that I had not seen in the garden before. It looked like a Song Thrush but was too big. I got my camera and was able to take some photographs of it. I then looked it up and found that it was a juvenile **Mistle Thrush.** It was a lovely bird. I wish I were able to get a better photo of it. It was a long way away, so this is the best I could get.

Mistle Thrush juvenile

Coal Tit

Nuthatch

In mid-August 2004, I saw for the first time a juvenile **Coal Tit**. I had only seen adults from October to March before.

At about the same time, a **Nuthatch** also visited for the first time. I did not want to scare it off and so did not attempt to take any photographs. I was fascinated by the way it always pointed head downwards when it was on the peanut feeder. It became a daily visitor after the first couple of weeks and was joined by another bird in September. After a while they seemed to take a liking for the sunflower hearts and thereafter rarely fed off the peanuts.

In October, I eventually got my chance to take some photographs of it and was pleased with the results. It is a very striking bird, one I was very pleased to see and watch in my garden.

The following year, 2005, I was really pleased to see these two young **Song Thrushes** on

Song Thrush...

my lawn during the first week of June. They were not the first Song Thrushes in the garden but were the first juveniles. I have read that this species is becoming scarce and hope that their dual appearance is a sign that they are doing well around this area.

A rare visitor is the **Wren.** They are one of my favourite birds and I found them fascinating as they dart about, gathering moss from the bricks on the raised flower bed. They never seem to stay still for a second and they are always on the go. This one showed up in the first week of January. It was the first time in two years I had seen one here, yet I have heard the male singing loudly. I kept my camera by the sofa to take advantage of every opportunity as it occurred, and eventually it did!

I have often seen a pair of **Red-legged Partridges** in the college grounds when coming back from an early morning walk with my dogs at the weekend, and at the front of

Wren

...juveniles

Red-legged Partridge

Adult Great Tit

the house during the day. One day in March I found them in my garden for the first time. I was lucky enough to get a couple of photos and some video footage before they went scurrying off into the field at the rear.

In early June I get a large number of **Blue** and **Great Tits** in my garden.

The **Great Tit,** the largest of the tit family, visits in large numbers. It is very striking with its black cap and bib, white cheeks and yellow breast (juvenile below).

The **Blue Tit** is the most common bird. I never get tired of seeing their antics, as of one holding a seed between its feet to eat it (below right), just like Coal, Marsh and Great Tits do. They are also very agile on the peanut feeder and hang upside down on the fat ball feeder.

At the beginning of that year, I had put a nest box up facing north-east in the quietest place in

Great Tit juvenile

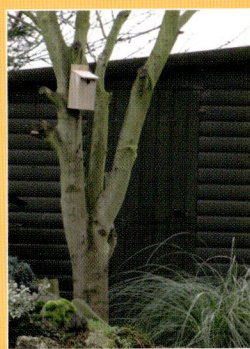

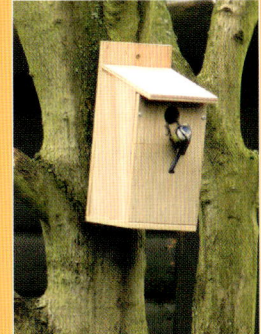

Nest boxes

my garden, as recommended by the RSPB. I had not thought to do so before, which is a bit strange considering my love of birds. After only one week, on the day of the RSPB Garden Bird Watch, I spotted two **Blue Tits** paying a lot of attention to the box. That was a good sign.

Already in the last week of May, the Blue Tits were very busy feeding their young in the nest box. I am not sure when they hatched exactly.

Blue Tit

Acrobatic Blue Tit

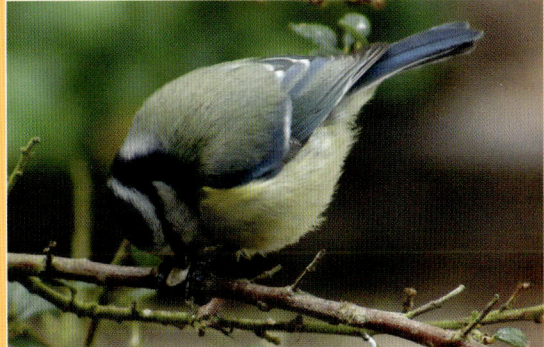

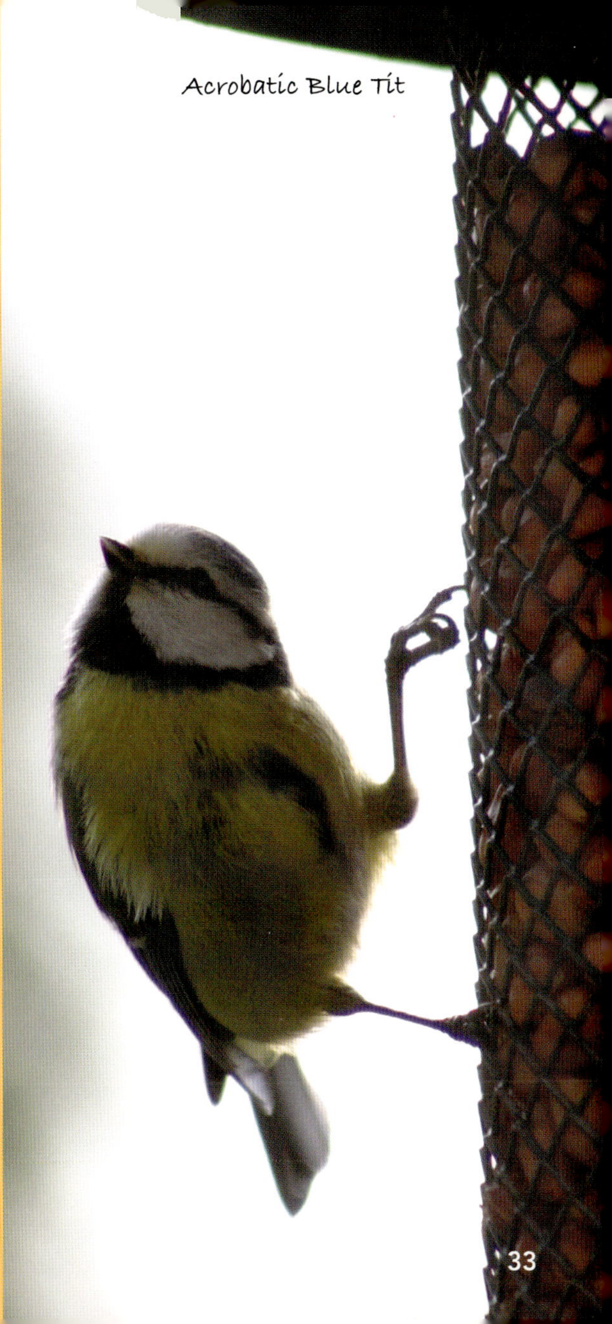

I took the photos of the birds flying from the nest on the 30th. I could not hear any noise from the young ones and assumed that they had hatched very recently.

By mid-June, the parent birds were feeding on average 30 times per hour a mixture of caterpillars, sunflower hearts and food from the lard balls. I have found that fledging takes place at about 18 days. Going from the date that they probably hatched, they should have fledged on or about the 16th June. A day later, I saw one of the young ones in the morning standing at the entrance hole. I thought that any moment it would fledge. It was 7:20am and I had to go to work but did not want to miss the birds leaving the nest. So I set up my camcorder at the window to record. This would give me an hour's recording and, hopefully, that would be long enough. When I got back from work, the parent birds were still taking caterpillars to the young in the nest box. I

looked at the video recording and within 15 minutes of the start I had managed to record two of the young leaving the nest (see below).

On the 18th June at 6:30am, I looked at the nest box to see a parent bird leave the nest. I had arranged to go out that day and so set the camcorder up again to record. On returning home, the video footage showed that the parent birds had visited the nest on three occasions. Each time they took a caterpillar and left the nest, still with the caterpillar. Thereafter they returned no more.

I could hear no sound from inside the box. Fearing the last of the young had died, I took the nest box down and removed the lid and was very happy to find that it was empty. The young ones must have left the nest in the early hours before I got up. As you can see from the photographs they look well. I have counted five in all.

Watching the Blue Tits fledge

I was really pleased with the outcome of my first nest box and wished that I had put one up long before. It makes up for the disappointment of the bumble bee nest box not being used. I hope to have better luck in the future. I have seen bats flying about so will put up some bat boxes as well and see what happens.

This **Sparrowhawk,** a female (females have brown-grey markings, whereas males are much smaller with blue-grey markings) had been coming to my garden daily throughout 2005. I had not been able to photograph it earlier as it's just a flash when it takes a bird and then flies off. Even if I was quick enough, I don't think it is the sort of photo I would like to get. However, one day in August that same year, she flew in and missed her prey and landed in the shrub above the patio. She remained there preening and so I quietly went upstairs and got my camera and was able to get several shots of her.

Female Sparrowhawk

Cute young Blue Tits

Female Sparrowhawk with close-up of head (inset)

Male Sparrowhawk (right)

It was lovely to watch her preening and observe the other birds as they harassed her. I think they must be safe as long as they can see her and get away should she attack. She stayed for about 20 minutes, so I had plenty of time to photograph and video her. She seemed happy to spend time in the garden quite often and her favourite perch was on the roof of the bird table. You can see from the photograph (left) that she was very relaxed and resting a leg, but constantly watching the other birds as they took food from the feeders.

Later, for a couple of months during the following year, I had daily glimpses of a Sparrowhawk as it swooped in to take a bird from one of the feeders. It is sad to dwell on this but Sparrowhawks have to live too. Then one day in December of 2006, he missed his prey and perched on the roof of the bird table (above). I was able to get this photograph of him, a magnificent male bird. I was really pleased to get this photograph as I now have very good illustrations of the difference between the male and female of the species.

The female on the far left has brown plumage and wide breast bars with a more yellow eye. The male is smaller, about three quarters the size of the female. The plumage on his back and wings are a blue-grey with chestnut bars on the breast and chestnut throat and cheeks and he has an orange eye.

I was able to take the photograph of a **Treecreeper** in March 2006. I noticed it on the oak tree at the front of the house and watched it for a good five minutes or so, then shot upstairs to get my camera. I had to change the lens from a 75 to 300mm and thought that it would be gone by the time I got downstairs to photograph it.

Luckily it hadn't. I had not realised that this species had such nice markings on back and wings. You can see how well adapted the curved beak is for getting the small insects on which it feeds from within the bark of the tree. It has very long claws for clinging to the tree as it works its way up before flying down to the bottom then working its way up again. As with all birds, it has to work hard to get its food and seems constantly on the go.

Collared Doves are one of my favourite garden birds. When I moved to the house I had just one pair visiting. Four years later, there were as many as four pairs at a time.

Treecreeper

Collared Dove

37

First male Great Spotted Woodpecker to be seen in the garden

I love to watch their antics to get from the roof of the bird table to the feeding platform. They slide down the roof and round to the side to get to the seeds. The big wide-spread fantail allows them to manoeuvre around. It was almost as if they were doing it in slow motion.

Since 2003, a male **Great Spotted Woodpecker** has regularly come into the garden. It was a bit of a challenge to photograph him, as he was very wary. As soon as he saw the camera he was off. I don't know, but I think it was the reflection from the lens that scared him away.

To get the photo on the left, I had to crawl into the lounge on all fours towards the sofa and gradually move the camera up to get the shot. It worked and I'm pleased with the result, although it would have been nice to get a photo of him on a tree, a more natural pose.

Amusingly, he used to land on the bottom of the framework around the patio windows, a support for climbing plants. He then gradually worked his way up to the top before moving on to the peanut feeder.

In the first week of August 2004, a juvenile of this woodpecker species came to the garden. It was on the fat ball feeder whilst its mum was on the peanut feeder. She was a lot more timid, and I was unable to get her photo. It was a shame, as she was a beautiful bird. The juvenile visited three or four times a day for about three weeks. Since then it has not

Juvenile Great Spotted Woodpecker

reappeared but I live in hope that it will return one day.

A year later, this Great Spotted Woodpecker – another male – appeared (right). He was a real character, very bold; he strutted around the garden as though he owned it. He came down the lawn, finding peanuts that the squirrels had buried, and then went to the bird table for his favourite sunflower hearts. After a drink from the bird bath, he finished with peanuts from the feeder. He was so much bolder than the female seen before and seemed so at home. I presume he was the juvenile also seen previously.

Throughout the early months of 2006, a male and female Great Spotted Woodpecker came to the garden several times a day. The male was a very striking bold bird and I was able to get photographs of him without too much trouble.

Second male Great Spotted Woodpecker to visit

Juvenile Great
Spotted Woodpecker

Robin

He would often come to the garden, take a peanut from the lawn, then go to the framework that held the shrub on the patio, wedge the peanut upright into a hole and hammer away at it. He would do this to four or five peanuts before feeding on the fat balls. Attempts to photograph the female, however, proved a complete failure as two years before. To this day, I have been unable to get a single shot as she is off as soon as she sees me.

In addition to the adult birds, a juvenile bird also later turned up and in contrast was very cooperative (top left). It came to the garden many times a day and one always knew when it was around as it was very verbal. I usually heard it long before I saw it and so was able to get ready to take photos and video the bird. I assumed it was the offspring of the adult pair referred to above. Another favourite haunt was the large oak tree at the front of the house. I was unable to get any photos of it there, however, as there was too much cover.

I only saw a **Green Woodpecker** in my garden once and would have loved to get a photo.

This bird, the **Robin,** is probably the most loved in anyone's garden. He was in and out of my garden regularly. On one occasion, I had three Robins in the garden and thought "Oh dear, I smell trouble", but am glad to say that my regular Robin saw the male intruder off. The third one I assume was his girlfriend as he seemed quite taken with her.

As you can see he is a handsome chap. He feeds mainly off scraps from the fat ball feeder. Every so often I treat him to some mealworms which he loves and scoffs immediately. He came to the bird bath of an evening just as it started to get dark. I assume he must have been very dirty as he was in it for a good few minutes, splashing around and seemingly having a lovely time. I think of all the birds he is the one that enjoys bath time most.

At the end of May 2006, this juvenile Robin (below right) came into the garden and sub-sequently became a regular visitor.

Jackdaws only started coming to the garden in September 2005. They are very timid birds. The slightest movement on my part and they were off and so I was unable to get any photographs of them earlier. They seem to visit the garden out of curiosity, wondering what's going on. In January 2006, the bird shown on page 42 arrived. It seemed a lot bolder and eventually I was able to get these photos of it.

Bath time for a robin and a shower for the sparrow...

Juvenile Robin

...and even more bathing.

Jackdaw

Siskin

I would love to know what makes some birds timid and others of the same species so bold. I am just glad of the latter as I get the opportunity to photograph them.

During the winter, **Siskins** are daily visitors but do not come in large flocks. The most I have seen at any one time is four. They leave for their breeding grounds in mid-March.

RSPB
Garden Bird Watch

On 29th-30th January 2005, the RSPB ran a Garden Bird Watch Weekend. They do this every year to see just how our garden birds are doing. In 2004, over 400,000 people helped count more than eight and a half million birds. I submitted my results online. In all, I spotted 25 species, totalling 86 birds: top was the Blue Tit

with 15 birds seen at once, followed by the House Sparrow with 14 birds. These sightings were taken on Sunday 30th January between 9:00 and 10:00 am. Unfortunately, I did not keep my results from the year before so I cannot tell how they are doing.

The results of the RSPB Big Garden Bird Watch for January 2006 were: total number of species 27; total number of birds 98. Top this year were 22 House Sparrows and 12 Black-birds. Blue Tits were down to 8 birds but I think they are generally up as a species. The count as a whole was up on last year, both in terms of the number of birds and species.

Blackbird, Collared Dove and Chaffinches

Mammals

This little **Hedgehog** has visited the garden nearly every night during September and October the year after I moved here. I would like to think it was the same one but I don't really know. It's surprising how quickly it moves as it searches for food all round the patio. You never know where it will turn up next. I leave it some dog food and water which it seems to enjoy.

In early April 2004, when I started putting peanuts out for the Pheasant, the Jays began eating them. At about 6:30 in the evening, I saw movement out of the corner of my eye. Looking to see what it might be and thinking that it moved mightily fast, and was possibly a bird, I saw a little head pop up. Then out of the hole it came, grabbing a peanut and shooting down again.

I had seen these holes before. There were two of them and I assumed that field mice had made them and that what I had just seen was a Field Mouse. I quickly got my camera, using the shelf of my coffee table as a tripod, and set it up ready for the mouse to come out again. I did not have to wait too long and out it popped and shot over to the peanuts. As luck would have it, as I could not get a very fast shutter speed due to the light fading (it was 1/15 second at f/5.6), it momentarily stopped with the peanut, just long enough to get a photo, then shot back home again. This ritual went on for some 15 to 20 minutes, each time stopping long enough for me to take a photo. I watched it for several days and eventually I was able to go outside and get to within 4ft of the hole and get some better pictures.

After looking it up in my trusty British wildlife field guide, I found out that it was actually a **Wood Mouse**, which is larger than the Field Mouse with much bigger ears and eyes. I have since seen it regularly. I do not know how many mice there were, but I do know that the one I saw and photographed is the same individual as it has a little nick out of his left ear. It seems to be the only one doing all the work. Surely it can't be eating *all* the peanuts on its own as it would get wedged in the hole! I know that pet mice only live for about 18 months; I am not sure about Wood Mice. I don't know the age of this one or how long it

Wood Mouse

45

Grey Squirrel

A very pregnant squirrel

will live. I will keep an eye open to see if there are any youngsters appearing in the future.

For my first year here I never saw a **Grey Squirrel** in the garden. Then one day in September 2002, I saw one – a male – hanging upside down from the framework on the patio, happily eating the sunflower hearts. It still surprises me how agile these creatures are. It has even found a way of unhooking the feeder and dropping it to the ground, then proceeding to drag it all the way to the bottom of the garden to eat in peace.

In February 2004, he was joined by a female. As you can see from the photo (below left), she looks heavily pregnant – or she has eaten too many sunflower hearts!

Foxes

I had seen evidence of foxes coming into my garden (i.e. faeces) for about 18 months, and seen dark shapes at my pond drinking and I had also seen foxes in the field at the back of the houses. In the middle of April 2004, all the apples and peanuts I had put on the ground for the birds disappeared overnight. It could only have been a fox, as it was too early in the year for the Hedgehog, and no way could the Wood Mouse eat all that food!

Subsequently, I bought a 500W light and fitted it to the framework on the patio. That evening, I switched it on before sunset so as not to

disturb anything after dark and waited. At about 9:15pm, down the garden he came. What a beautiful sight: a young male fox. He went right up to where the peanuts and apples were and started eating. I put my camera to my eye and focused. He was very timid and wary and was put off by the seed feeder swinging above his head. Just as I was about to take his photo he ran off. I was disappointed at not getting a shot, but even so was thrilled at having seen him and was more determined than ever to get a photograph of him. I named him White Tip due to his prominent white tail marking.

The following day, I set up my camera on a tripod, with the lens as close as possible to the patio window, closed the curtains and pinned them around the lens. I moved the bird feeder that disturbed him the night before, turned the light on before sunset and again waited. I had to look through the camera lens as this was the only way to see out into the garden. Close to midnight I was still waiting in anticipation and feeling sure that he would turn up, as I had put some dog food out for him. Just then White Tip appeared. He walked down the garden towards the food. He started eating immediately, lifting his head and looking around as if mistrusting this offering of food, maybe thinking it was some kind of trap. Moving the bird feeder away seemed to have made a difference. I watched him for some minutes before trying to take a photograph. He was not looking as good as he had the night before as it was now raining and he was wet and dirty. Then I discovered a problem with the lighting as I could not use a flash. The light from the 500W lamp was fine for watching the fox. With the camera set to maximum 3200 ISO, I was only getting a 1/15 second shutter speed at maximum aperture of f/5.6 using the 480mm lens (that is far too slow for taking a photo with any movement in it). The fox was constantly on the go, eating and looking around. I had to find a way of getting him to stop for the second it took to take the photo. I have been told that making a loud kissing sound on the back of your hand would get the attention of a fox. Nothing to lose, I gave it a try. Hay presto! It worked! ... I took a dozen or more photographs. White Tip stayed for about 20 minutes and, after finishing all the food, trotted off and out into the fields. It was a magical moment, one I will always treasure. I have enlarged the two best photos and pinned them on my kitchen wall!

White Tip

I now put food out for him every night. It is always gone by the time I get up in the morning. I have actually seen him a couple of times since. Assuming he remains well, I am sure I will see more of him in the autumn and winter with the longer nights. In the mean time, I continue to feed him, look at his photos and remember that initial brief encounter.

The garden was visited by what I thought was a single fox throughout that year, his favourite treat being peanuts. In the first week of October, he came into my garden as usual but I thought he looked different. On closer inspection, I noticed that he had different markings on his face, the black marking on either side of his snout did not extend up to just below his eyes. Then on the following night I saw yet another fox. I knew this was a different one as it had no white tip to its tail. During November and December, foxes visited every night. My friend Clive told me that his dad put eggs out for his foxes and that they loved them. I must confess I thought he was pulling my leg but now I get through two dozen eggs a week.

One night in November, yet another new fox visited my garden; he seemed older than the others and fuller in the face. I named him Basil as he reminded me of Basil Brush. The following night, Basil came to my garden and was eating the peanuts but, at the same time, seemed very uneasy, looking around and cowering. I could not tell what was wrong. After a few minutes, he stopped eating, turned and went behind some shrubs by the fence. He lay very flat and made a

Basil

49

strange noise, when suddenly another fox came down the lawn. He charged into the shrubs repeatedly, scent marking and rolling on the ground … which they do to disguise their own scent. After a minute or two it left and Basil remained hiding in the shrubs for another 10 to 15 minutes. When he felt it was safe to do so he left the garden without eating again. Twenty minutes after Basil had left, White Tip returned. He came in along the fence behind the shrubs to where Basil had been hiding, sniffed around and then fed on the peanuts.

Throughout November and December six different foxes came into the garden, amongst them Patch.

In January the next year (2005), I had a further two new foxes visiting. Half Tail, which has only

Gemini, the vixen

Patch

50

White Tip with scar nearly gone

Half Tail

half a tail and also has very short legs, came first; he's a little cutie. A week later Gemini (with twin spots on her tail) visited for the first time.

One day that same January, I saw White Tip lying down eating, his face black and cut. I was not sure what had happened to him. It must have been on that day, as the night before when I had photographed him he was perfectly well. When he got up to go he could not put weight on his right hind leg. I feared he had been hit by a car and must have broken his leg. He returned the following night and was no better. I was somewhat concerned whether he would survive. The following day I put some chicken legs out for him, hoping he would find them before the others. He did and was always the first each night to get more than his fair share. My friend Debbie got some packs of chicken wings (14 to a pack) and I put a whole pack

out each night. White Tip would come, sit down, eat one and then take two away. I assume he hid them before coming back for another two or three. It could not have been a broken leg, as after a couple of weeks he was looking a lot better, if not a bit tatty where his fur was missing on his face. He only had a slight limp now and looked a lot brighter two weeks later. I discontinued the free chicken meals as I didn't want him to get too dependent on handouts and hence not hunt for himself. He still enjoys coming in for some peanuts though.

By February, White Tip had fully recovered. On occasions, he would come to the garden with Gemini. She was looking a bit plumper (I do not think it was all down to the chicken). I was keeping my fingers crossed and hoped to be able to report and photograph some cubs over the coming weeks.

White Tip enjoying the peanuts

In the first week in May, White Tip came to the garden for some eggs. It was the first time I'd seen him in over a month. He had the eggs first then some peanuts; foxes seem to really enjoy them.

Shortly after starting on the peanuts, White Tip was joined by a younger looking fox, another vixen; he looked at her and continued eating. He seems very relaxed with her. Could this be his mate? I have called her Honey.

On June 11th, I got up early, hoping for a change to get some photos of a fox in daylight. I did not have to wait too long. Honey arrived at about 6:15am. She seemed to like the raisins I had put out for the birds.

Within 15 minutes of Honey's departure, Half Tail arrived. It was good to see him as he had not appeared in over a month. He too liked the raisins.

The reason the foxes looked so wet and dirty is that they have had to come across the hay fields at the back of the garden, which had not yet been cut. In Half Tail's case, this meant that the grass was taller than he, his legs seeming even shorter in daylight.

I was at the window taking these photographs and shooting some video for the monthly video diary. It was obvious they could see me, but did not seem too worried. They would just stop eating and look at me to see if I moved and then would continue eating. One night I was shooting

Honey and White Tip

These are two new foxes in my garden: Nelson above and Misty below

Half Tail

Honey

Fox cubs in the garden

some video of Honey with the patio doors wide open. Again she could see me. She would stop and move a yard or so away if I moved or made the slightest sound, whereafter she would come back and continue eating. It was great being so close to her with nothing between us. I felt I could reach out and stroke her, although I would not want the foxes to get that friendly, as this would put them in danger with other people who may not like them.

Honey returned to the garden all through the first months and in March I felt sure she was pregnant. I did not see her during the first weeks of April. Then on the 24th, she appeared and, as you can see from the photo, looks as though she has had her cubs. She came every day from then on and I was hoping one day that she would bring her cubs with her. Unfortunately, she didn't that day.

However, on July 25th at 2:45 in the morning, I was awoken by loud screeching noises coming from the garden. I thought that a fox may have got one of the neighbour's cats. I went down-stairs and put the garden light on. I walked into the living room and to my surprise saw six foxes. There was Half Tail who I hadn't seen for months and five cubs that looked like they could be about three months old. Could they be Honey's offspring? I watched them for about 15 minutes then realised I was not getting any film footage so immediately went and got my camera. I was thus lucky enough to video them and get a dozen or so stills but could not get all the foxes all together (a bit of a tall order).

Cubs at play

Small Tortoiseshell

Butterflies and Moths

During 2005, in order to attract more butterflies and moths, I let the stinging nettles and other wild plants grow at the bottom of the garden. They are behind the bamboo so it doesn't look untidy.

Butterflies

The **Large White** is a regular visitor, its flight period extending from May to September.

Below, a pair of Large White butterflies is courting. The female has two spots on top as well as on the undersides of the wings, whereas the male has two spots on the undersides of the wings only.

Large White

Once the Buddleia is in bloom (July-August), the **Small Tortoiseshell** is a regular visitor. According to my field guide, the species is on the wing from March to October. I have not seen it in my garden before July. The caterpillars live on the nettles.

Large White butterflies courting

Small Tortoiseshell caterpillars

Painted Lady

Peacock

The **Painted Lady** is another butterfly that visits from July to September when the Buddleia is in bloom.

The **Peacock** is the most common butterfly to visit the garden. I have seen it in the spring after hibernation. Adults fly from March to September. Their caterpillars feed on Common Nettle.

The **Red Admiral** is one of my favourite butterflies. A small number of adults may hibernate but generally it is a summer migrant to Great Britain. I get a lot in my garden from July to August. Caterpillars also feed on Common Nettle.

The **Comma** butterfly is a rare visitor to the garden. I have only seen this butterfly about

Red Admiral

Comma

Gatekeeper female

Meadow Brown

five or six times in the three years I have been here. In the photograph you can see the white comma on the underside of the wing, which gives it its name. It is another species that hibernates, flying from March to September. Caterpillars feed on Common Nettle, elm and hops.

The **Gatekeeper**, flying during July and August, lives at the back of the shed, feeding on the flowers of bramble. The caterpillars feed on grass.

This is a **Meadow Brown** (right). I have so far been unable to take a photograph of it with its wings open, but will keep trying!

Common Blue

The **Common Blue** flies in June and July and is seen frequently, as its name suggests. Since it flies very fast, I spent a lot of time trying to get this photograph.

The **Large Skipper** flies in June and July. I have only seen this butterfly once in my garden. It was on my poppies in July 2002 and stayed around for about half an hour, long enough for me to take some good photographs.

I saw the rather tatty **Speckled Wood** (below) in the garden for the first time in June 2004. A widespread woodland butterfly, it flies from April to September. Its caterpillars feed on grasses.

Large Skipper

Speckled Wood

Magpie moth

Silver-ground Carpet Moth

Moths

The **Magpie** moth flies from July to August. I have only seen this moth in my garden on one occasion – in July 2001. A common and widespread moth; it flies from July to August.

Silver-ground Carpet Moth. I have seen this moth on many occasions on the vegetation around the pond, on the odd occasion even in the house. They fly from May to August and are widespread and common in grassy areas. Their larvae feed on bedstraw.

In late June 2002, strolling through my garden, I saw something bright yellow out of the corner of my eye and thought it was a Brimstone butterfly. It turned out to be a

Brimstone Moth. It was a blustery day and I assume it was blown out of its roost by the wind. I looked it up in my field guide that said

Brimstone Moth

Scalloped Oak moth

that they were often common and fly from April to October. As yet this is the only sighting I have had and am glad I was able to photograph it.

I saw the **Scalloped Oak** moth for the first time in July 2005. It flies from June to August and is widespread and fairly common in woodland. Larvae feed on many deciduous trees and shrubs.

One evening in the middle of April 2005, I found an **Emperor Moth**. It is a day-flying species (April to May). This one is a female; the male is a little smaller and much browner. They have a wingspan of 50-60mm; the adults do not feed. The female flies at dusk to lay her eggs, as this one is doing. The male flies by day, searching for the female's scent with his feathery antennae. I will have to keep a look out for the caterpillars which are very showy and feed on a variety of plants, including heather and bramble.

Emperor Moth

Pug moth upperside

I saw this moth (below) on my patio door and was able to get these photos from above and below. It is a **pug moth**, but I am not sure exactly which species it is. It's good to be able to see it from both sides.

This is a **Peppered Moth** (right) and I saw it for the first time in June 2005 on the wall by the patio. It is common and widespread in England, Wales and Ireland, flying from May to August. It favours woods and gardens. Larvae feed on a wide range of plants.

Poplar Hawk-moth. I saw this moth on the wall in the garden. At rest the grey-brown forewings obscure the reddish marks on the hindwings; these are exposed if the moth becomes alarmed. It normally rests by day among leaves and is easily overlooked. It is seen from May to August. The caterpillar is bright green and has diagonal stripes along the body, with a horn at the tail end. It feeds on poplar and willow.

Peppered Moth

Poplar Hawk-moth

Pug moth underside

63

Confronting a Large Red Damselfly

More insects and Spiders

Dragon- and damselflies

The **Large Red Damselfly** is the first damselfly seen around my pond. It appears in early May, and flies to late August.

This is followed by the **Common Blue Damselfly**, which appears in late May/early June, flying to early September.

The best time to photograph damselflies is when they are mating as they will settle on waterside vegetation for longer periods. When they are on their own they tend to fly off when approached with a camera.

Common Blue Damselflies mating, with male above

Large Red Damselfly

Southern Hawker dragonfly. In early June 2003, I was standing near the pond ready and rearing to photograph anything interesting when I noticed something on one of the plants in the water. I was able to get a good look at it through my macro lens. It was the empty case of a nymph. It was the first time I had ever seen one. It is really ugly compared with the beautiful insect that emerges from it (left). I saw several more over the next two weeks.

Subsequently, I visited the pond at different times hoping to see a dragonfly emerge, but was never successful. I think they must hatch very early in the morning. If I see some this year I will try and get up early enough to watch them emerge. This would be a wonderful thing to witness. It would also be a great opportunity to photograph the dragonfly before it becomes too active.

Southern Hawker nymphal cases

Common Darter

Seven-spot Ladybird and its larva on a rose (left)

Shown above is another dragonfly that visits my garden and is probably the **Common Darter**. It is often the latest flying species of dragonfly, flying from June to late autumn.

Beetles

Seven-spot Ladybird. I need a lot of these in my garden as I get a lot of greenfly. I found its larva on a rose; it's the first time I had ever seen one.

The **Cardinal Beetle** is so called because of its colour. In sunny weather, it visits flowers to hunt for small insects.

Cardinal Beetle

67

The **Cockchafer** is commonly called the May-bug as it is most often found in May or early June. The larvae feed on plant roots and can sometimes be a serious pest of farm and garden crops, whereas the adult beetle eats the foliage of deciduous trees but is not considered a serious pest like the larvae. One evening in the first week of June 2006, at around 10:30pm, I heard a loud buzzing sound coming from outside on the patio. I went out and found this Cockchafer. It's the first time I had seen one in my garden and so was very pleased to get some photographs of it.

Not exactly pretty but fascinating all the same.

I have not been able to identify this **ladybird** from any of my reference books. The nearest one is the **22-spot Ladybird** but the present specimen has around 18 and is more cream-coloured than yellow, as in the 14-spot Ladybird.

Cockchafer

Unidentified Ladybird

Water beetle

Carabid ground beetle

I found this tiny **water beetle** on the leaf of a water plant in the pond, mid-June 2006.

This **Carabid ground beetle** seems just as at home in the water (right) as it does out of it (above right), but in fact it is a terrestrial predator feeding on other insects, worms, slugs and snails.

In Irish mythology the **Devil's Coach-horse** beetle is a symbol of corruption, able to kill simply on sight. It is said that the Devil's Coach-horse will appear after dealing with the Devil and that it will eat sinners. On raising its tail it casts a curse. In reality, it is a predatory beetle with a powerful pair of mandibles (jaws) for eating small creatures such as spiders, caterpillars and earwigs. I found this beetle by the compost heap. When I went near it to get the photograph it curled up its abdomen over its body and opened its jaws. They do this when threatened; unfortunately, it did not hold that pose long enough to get a photograph.

Devil's Coach-horse

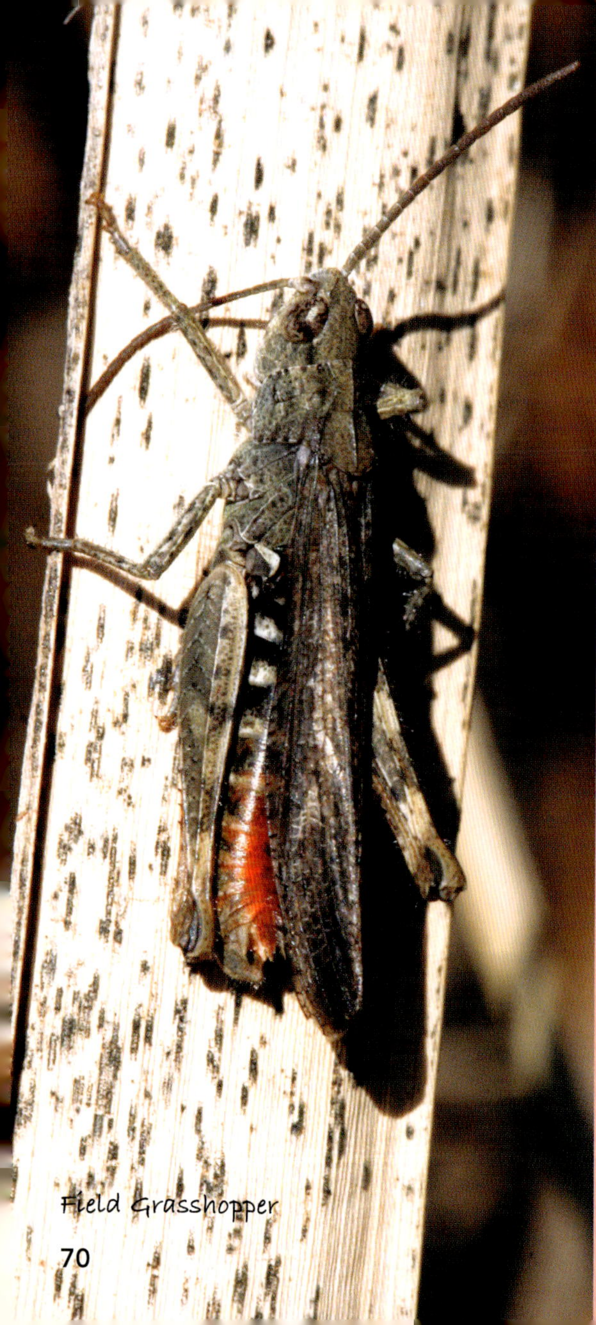

Field Grasshopper

Dark Bush-cricket nymph

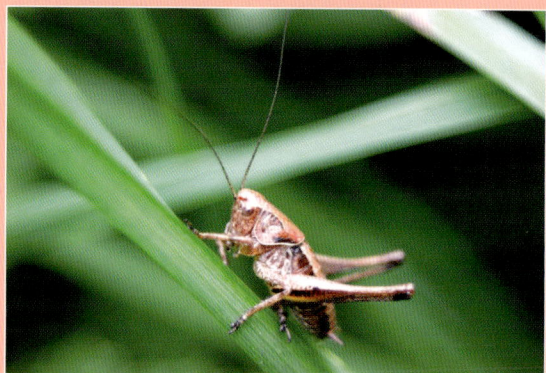

Crickets and grasshoppers

The easiest way to distinguish between a grasshopper and a cricket is that grasshoppers have short antennae whereas crickets have long antennae.

This is the nymph (above) of a **Dark Bush-cricket**. I do not get a lot of them in the garden.

The **Oak Bush-cricket** (above right) is a pale green species that lives in trees, typically oak, where it feeds on small insects after dark. Males sing by drumming with a hind foot on the leaf. I have seen these crickets in the house several times.

The **Field Grasshopper** (left) frequents woodland margins and dry, grassy places.

Oak Bush-cricket

The photograph is of a male as it has a red tip to the abdomen. The females are green on top of the head and pronotum.

True Flies

St. Mark's Fly is named so because the adult often appears around St. Mark's day (April 25th). I saw the two on the right mating at the beginning of May 2005.

The males fly with dangling legs as you can see in the photo above right. They are found in areas of short grass and the larvae live in the ground on rotting vegetation.

This is a **House Fly**, freshly hatched whose cuticle has yet to harden. It landed on my patio window on the 19th March, 2005.

St. Mark's Fly

House Fly

Flesh fly

Bluebottle fly

Hover-fly

Greenbottle fly

Hover-fly

This **flesh fly** (far left), one of several red-eyed species with large feet, breeds in carrion and may investigate dustbins, although rarely enters the house.

The **Bluebottle** fly and the **Common Greenbottle** are two other species which lay their eggs on carrion for the larva to feed off. The latter species is used for maggot therapy to clean infected wounds.

Brightly coloured **hover-flies** are the most easily recognised of all the flies due to their often wasp-like or bee-like appearance (see page 79) and their ability to hover. They can move in all directions, including backwards, and can hold a fixed position in the air even in windy conditions. There are many thousands of species worldwide.

I saw this hover-fly, *Volucella pellucens*, (right) in my garden for the first time on the 30th May, 2005. The first thing I noticed was the brilliant white band around its middle. I must get a more comprehensive book on insects so that I can identify other new flies that are turning up in the garden (it may well be that they have always been there or I am being more observant, who knows).

Another fly, the **Yellow Dung-fly** (p.74), was seen on the outside of the patio window. The photograph is taken from the inside, giving an unusual view of the fly. This

Volucella pellucens

Yellow Dung-fly

Yellow Dung-fly

Phantom midge

made identification difficult, until I found one on the lupins in the garden.

This (right) is a **phantom midge**. Again this was on my patio window. This midge doesn't bite humans. It breeds in all kinds of still water, including garden ponds and water butts.

The photograph was taken with my new Sigma 150mm macro lens. It is an excellent medium telephoto lens as well as being a 1:1 life-size macro. I am very pleased with it and hope to get a lot more of the smaller wildlife around the garden.

The photos on the far right are again of a fly seen on the patio window, photographed on the 31st May 2005. It is a **Crane-fly**; adults are seen in spring and summer. I do not remember ever seeing crane-flies at this time of year before (I have always associated seeing them in September). Look at its green eyes!

Dance Fly

The **Dance Fly** (Empididae) has excellent eyesight. Its legs are strong and bristly and it is predatory on other smaller flies. It also will take nectar from flowers and during courtship undergoes strange rituals in which the male offers the female a nuptual gift, often a dead insect. Despite its menacing proboscis used to feed on its prey it doesn't bite humans.

This **Bee-fly** visits flowers to feed on nectar. Note the very long proboscis to enable it to get to the nectar. Its larvae predate grubs of solitary bees and wasps in their underground nests.

Bee-fly

Crane-fly: Note halteres, gyroscopic balancing knobs for flight (inset)

75

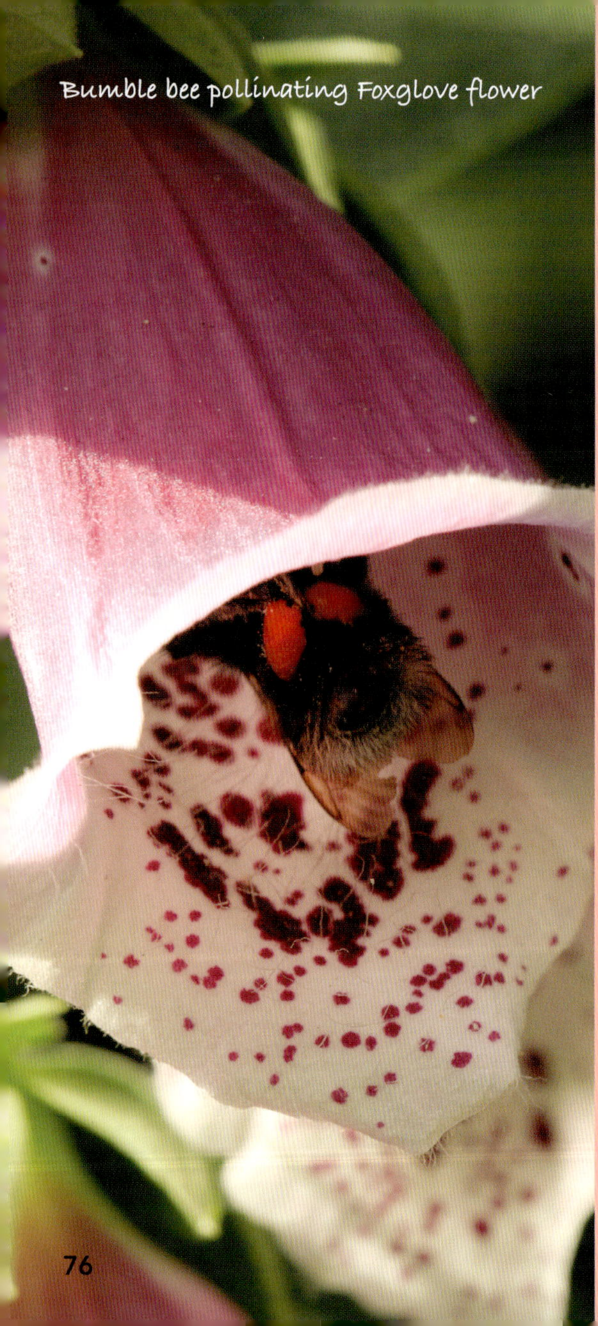

Bumble bee pollinating Foxglove flower

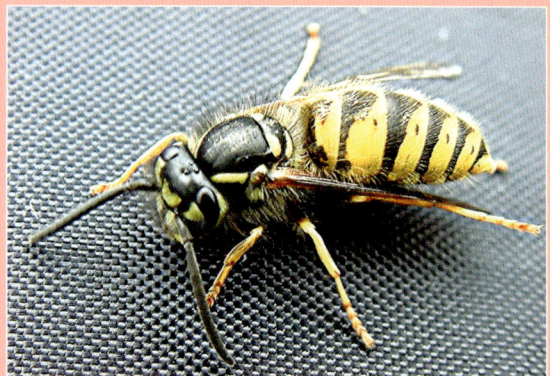

Common Wasp

Wasps, Bees and Sawflies

Common Wasp. In the spring and summer, the wasp is a friend to gardeners as they kill large numbers of pests such as sawflies and aphids to feed their own larvae. Only in the autumn do they get a sweet tooth and become a nuisance and may occasionally sting. Unlike bees, wasps have an unbarbed sting and can use it several times.

The **Hornet**, the largest British wasp, had until the last 20 years or so almost disappeared from the south-east and central England, possibly due to persecution and loss of habitat. I have often seen hornets in the garden but they rarely stay still long enough to photograph them. One early June morning

Hornet

Hornet

in 2006, I was in my kitchen and nearly trod on something. Taking a closer look, I found it to be a Hornet. I carefully picked it up in a tumbler and put it out in the garden. It stayed around long enough, I'm pleased to say, to get these pictures.

I saw this wasp (right) in June 2005 on the wall in the garden. As you can see, it is by a hole (an old plastic wall plug) with something in its mouth that looks like a piece of mud. It went into the hole and left the mud in there. Initially, I could not find any wasp in my books that fitted the exact description of this one. The nearest is the **Mason Wasp**. The individual cells are stocked with beetle larvae, caterpillars and spiders, immobilised by its paralysing sting; these are fed upon by the developing wasp larvae. The bricks in this wall are quite flaky and sandy, but the ready-made holes save digging. There are other old plugholes

Mason Wasp

that have been filled in. I did check these the following spring but unfortunately missed the hatchlings.

I have looked into the hole below and it does look like there is a dead fly in there.

Borage – bees love it!

A hover-fly, mimicking a honey bee

White-tailed Bumble Bee

There are many species of bee in my garden. One is the **White-tailed Bumble Bee** (note the long tongue to probe for nectar).

There are also many **Honey Bees** in my garden (below right). I was able to visit a friend who has beehives. He showed me how the honey is collected, and said that the bees will travel up to 2 miles to collect pollen. His hives are only about a mile away so the honey bees in my garden may well be his.

This worker bee (left) is fanning for signalling other workers or to cool the hive.

Red Mason Bees are a docile species and are safe with children and pets. They are excellent pollinators of fruit trees, raspberries, strawberries and are fond of a range of flowers and tree blossom. In mid-April 2004, I bought a nest for the Red Mason Bees and fixed it onto a south-facing fence so that it was warm and sunny. I kept the soil below moist.

The bee lays an egg in the end of one of the tubes and seals it with a plug of moist soil. When the end of the tube is plugged with mud the tube is full. At the end of September, the full tubes are stored at a temperature of ~4°C in a fridge, or wrapped in newspaper and stored in an unheated shed. In the following early spring, say the last week in March, the tubes are put back into the plastic cylinder, just before flowering begins. Other bees that may use the nest tubes are the Blue Mason Bees in mid-summer. These bees use chewed leaves to seal their nest rather than mud. At the same time, two or three species of leaf-cutter bee might also be attracted. They seal their nests with discs of cut leaves.

Since putting the nest tubes in the garden for the mason bees in 2004, there has not been a single bee using them – until now, that is July 2006, when this **leaf-cutter bee** started to lay eggs (above right). You can see the leaf plug on the tube next to the one being filled.

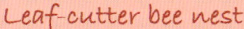
Leaf-cutter bee nest

You can also see what neat plugs the chewed-up leaves make and also just make out the bee leaving the nest (arrow).

A year later, at the end of January 2005, I put a bumble bee nest box in the garden. I placed it in the position that was recommended, low down facing south but out of direct sunlight. Clean hay is supplied for nesting material; it is suggested that an old

Bumble bee nest box

Red Mason Bee nest

Turnip Sawfly

Hawthorn Shield Bug

Common Earwig

Greenfly (Aphids)

mouse nest is ideal as bumble bees are attracted by the smell.

I was able to get some old mouse nesting material from work and am now hoping that the nest is being used. The box has a hinged lid with a Perspex cover below it. This will provide me with the ideal opportunity to photograph what goes on inside the nest.

This is a **Turnip Sawfly** (far left). Sawflies are not flies but are closely related to bees and wasps.

Other insects

The insect pictured (below far left) is a female **Common Earwig**. The pincer-like cerci at the tail end are more curved in the male.

The **Hawthorn Shield Bug** feeds mainly on hawthorn berries but also feeds on leaves of other deciduous trees when berries are not available.

There have been a lot of **greenfly** this year (2005). I do not spray them as I don't want to harm the wildlife, and there seems to be more ladybirds about. I think this is why the greenfly haven't had a detrimental effect on the garden plants.

Each antenna of the **Squash Bug** has four segments (instead of five in the shield bugs). It lives on waste ground and in hedgerows.

Male Common Scorpion Fly

Pictured above is a **Pond Skater** going for its dinner. You can see how they use their legs to spread their weight over the water surface to prevent them from sinking.

I saw this insect (left) on the plants by the pond in June 2005. It's the first time I had ever seen anything like it; it looks almost prehistoric. It is a **Common Scorpion Fly**, actually a member of the Order Mecoptera, not Diptera, which are the true flies. It lives in cool, moist places and feeds on dead or dying insects. This is a male, the large genitalia being clearly visible; the female has a pointed abdomen. It is, surprisingly, most related to the fleas!

A Snipe-fly from above...

...and from below

Below left and right you see a **Snipe-fly**, *Rhagio* sp., a true fly, which bears similarity to the female Scorpion Fly. As it was sitting on the windowpane it gave me the great opportunity to photograph it from both sides.

Spiders

The **European Garden Spider** is the most common spider in my garden. This orb web spider will wait at the centre of its web, facing down, for an insect to be trapped, then will bite and paralyse it. She will then wrap it in silk and inject it with enzymes to turn its body tissues into a liquid soup for drinking.

I think this is a type of **Wolf Spider**, a *Paradosa* sp., (p.86) and was seen for the first time in May 2005. I have logs around the front of the pond and found several of these spiders under the bark. They are very fast moving and it was difficult to get the photographs.

Garden Spider from above and (inset) from below

Garden Spider at work

Wolf Spider

A long-legged spider

Facing a Wolf Spider

I managed to get these photographs of the spider in April 2006.

This **long-legged spider** (above) has been seen around the pond regularly. It is, like the garden spider, an araneid, an orb web spider, probably a *Metellina* sp.

The spider in the photo right above could be mistaken for a crab spider, but in fact it is again an **orb web spider**, possibly a *Metellina* sp. It

An orb web spider with a fly for dinner

looks like it has caught a fly for dinner and already wrapped it up in silk.

Harvestmen

Harvestmen resemble spiders and are recognised by their small round body and very long legs. They occur in late summer, sometimes seen walking over bare earth in harvest fields.

Harvestman

I am not sure what this spider is from this angle but thought it made a nice photograph with the dew on the web

Frogs, Snakes, Slugs and Snails

Frogs

Frogs arrive at my pond in late March - early April. This seems a little late compared with a friend's pond where frogs spawn can be found as early as the first week of March. Since he lives in Enfield, the climate there may be a bit warmer, which may account for the difference. I had a very successful frog-breeding season in 2003. There were so many young ones that, before mowing the lawn, I had to go round to get them out of the way. My greenhouse was their favourite retreat. It was fascinating to see how quickly they grew.

The next year, however, I didn't see a single youngster. Up until August 2003, I had no fish in my pond. When my friends from Potters Bar moved up to Northumberland, they could not take their two very large carp with them and so we put both fish in my pond. As usual I looked out early one morning in late March 2004: the water in the pond looked like it was boiling. I counted six mating pairs of frogs. They laid spawn in the pots of the irises and rushes. I kept a close eye on the developing tadpoles, which were doing well. One morning I went down and they were all gone. From time to time I spotted the odd tadpole but do not know if any

Princely profile

Tadpoles

developed into frogs. I will have to put a barrier round the area with the spawn so as to prevent the fish getting to the tadpoles and hope that all will be well for them in the future.

Snakes

It was a hot June afternoon in 2003 and I had just got home after taking my dogs for a walk. As I normally do when I get back, I went out into the garden just to see if there was anything new going on. I was looking into the pond and glanced over to the waterfall. At the bottom of it, I saw something jutting out and could not

Common Frog on the move

Waterfall in the garden pond

make out what it was, so I got a bit closer for a better look. It was a snake! I was very surprised as I had never seen one before locally. I quickly ran indoors to get my camera, all the time thinking it unlikely to be there when I got back, but was pleasantly surprised to see that it was in exactly the same place.

I'm no expert on snakes but I was sure by the markings on its head and the fact that it was near the water that it was a **Grass Snake** and not an Adder. On looking it up later in my field guide, I found out that it was indeed a Grass Snake. I was very impressed with the speed with which it swam around the pond.

Grass Snake

The diet of these snakes consists of tadpoles, frogs and fish. I knew that my fish would be okay as they are far too big for it, but I could not say the same for the many frogs that abounded. This was the only time I was to see it, so I assume that it had its fill and found a more plentiful supply of food somewhere else. I kept an eye on my compost heap just in case it laid some eggs, as I know that is where they are likely to lay them, but no young appeared.

Slugs and Snails

In addition to frogs and the said snake, my garden also boasts a variety of beautiful slugs and snails – very colourful and hence as you see, very photogenic – despite the damage they do to my beloved lupins and other plants.

Field Slug

A yellow slug, possibly Deroceras agreste

Brown-lipped Snail

Brown-lipped Snail on window

Amber Snail

Common Garden Snail

Probably a White-lipped Snail

93

Bibliography

Paul Sterry, 1997,
Collins Complete British Wildlife Photoguide, Harper Collins

George C. McGavin, 2005,
Insects and Spiders (Pocket Nature), Dorling Kindersley Ltd.

Reader's Digest, 2004,
Field Guide to the Butterflies and other Insects of Britain, The Reader's Digest Association Ltd.

Michael Chinery, 1986,
Collins Guide to the Insects of Britain and Western Europe, Collins

Useful Websites

www.ukbutterflies.co.uk
www.ukmoths.org.uk
www.dragonflysoc.org.uk
www.abdn.ac.uk/mammal
www.amentsoc.org
www.rspb.org.uk
www.bto.org
www.royensoc.co.uk
www.thebhs.org
www.wildlifetrust.org.uk/herts/
www.wildaboutbritain.co.uk

Wildlife biodiversity in my garden as documented during 2001-06:

Birds

Blackbird (*Turdus merula*)
Long-tailed Tit (*Aegithalos caudatus*)
Mallard (*Anas platyrhynchos*)
Goldcrest (*Regulus regulus*)
Song Thrush (*Turdus philomelos*)
Pied Wagtail (*Motacilla alba*)
Goldfinch (*Carduelis carduelis*)
Chaffinch (*Fringilla coelebs*)
Dunnock (*Prunella modularis*)
House Sparrow (*Passer domesticus*)
Greenfinch (*Carduelis chloris*)
Grey Heron (*Ardea cinerea*)
Pheasant (*Phasianus colchicus*)
Magpie (*Pica pica*)
Starling (*Sturnus vulgaris*)
Jay (*Garrulus glandarius*)
Marsh Tit (*Poecile palustris*)
Linnet (*Carduelis cannabina*)
Wood Pigeon (*Columba palumbus*)
Little Owl (*Athene noctua*)
Carrion Crow (*Corvus corone*)
Mistle Trush (*Turdus viscivorus*)
Coal Tit (*Periparus ater*)
Nuthatch (*Sitta europaea*)
Wren (*Troglodytes troglodytes*)
Red-legged Partridge (*Alectoris rufa*)
Blue Tit (*Cyanistes caeruleus*)
Great Tit (*Parus major*)
Sparrowhawk (*Accipiter nisus*)
Treecreeper (*Certhia familiaris*)
Collared Dove (*Streptopelia decaocto*)
Great Spotted Woodpecker (*Dendrocopos major*)
Green Woodpecker (*Picus viridis*)
Robin (*Erithacus rubecula*)
Jackdaws (*Corvus monedula*)
Siskin (*Carduelis spinus*)

Mammals

Hedgehog (*Erinaceus europaeus*)
Wood Mouse (*Apodemus sylvaticus*)
Grey Squirrel (*Sciurus carolinensis*)
Red Fox (*Vulpes vulpes*)

Insects

Butterflies

Large White (*Pieris brassicae*)
Small Tortoiseshell (*Aglais urticae*)
Painted Lady (*Vanessa cardui*)
Peacock (*Inachis io*)
Red Admiral (*Vanessa atalanta*)
Comma (*Polygonia c-album*)
Gatekeeper (*Pyronia tithonus*)
Meadow Brown (*Maniola jurtina*)
Common Blue (*Polyommatus icarus*)
Large Skipper (*Ochlodes sylvanus*)
Speckled Wood (*Pararge aegeria*)

Moths

Magpie (*Abraxas grossulariata*)
Silver-ground Carpet Moth (*Xanthorhoe montanata*)
Brimstone Moth (*Opisthograptis luteolata*)
Scalloped Oak (*Crocallis elinguaria*)
Emperor Moth (*Saturnia pavonia*)
Peppered Moth (*Biston betularia*)
Poplar Hawk-moth (*Laothoe populi*)

Damsel- and Dragonflies

Large Red Damselfly (*Pyrrhosoma nymphula*)
Common Blue Damselfly (*Enallagma cyathigerum*)
Southern Hawker (*Aeshna cyanea*)
Common Darter (*Sympetrum striolatum*)

Beetles

Seven-spot Ladybird (*Coccinella 7-punctata*)
Cardinal Beetle (*Pyrochroa serraticornis*)
Cockchafer (*Melolontha melolontha*)
22-spot Ladybird (*Thea 22-punctata*)
A water beetle (probably *Enochrus testaceus*)
Carabid ground beetle (probably a *Pterostichus* sp.)
Devil's Coach-horse (*Staphylinus olens*)

Crickets and grasshoppers

Dark Bush-cricket (*Pholidoptera griseoaptera*)
Oak Bush-cricket (*Meconema thalassinum*)
Field Grasshopper (*Chorthippus brunneus*)

Other insects

St. Mark's Fly (*Bibio marci*)
House Fly (*Musca domestica*)
Continued ➤

Continued ➤

Flesh fly (*Sarcophaga* sp.)
Bluebottle (*Calliphora vomitoria*)
Greenbottle (*Lucilia sericata*)
Two unidentified hover-flies (Family Syrphidae)
Hover-fly (*Volucella pellucens*)
Yellow Dung-fly (*Scathophaga stercoraria*)
Phantom Midge (*Chaoborus* sp.)
Crane-fly (*Tipula oleracia*)
Dance Fly (Empididae)
Bee-fly (*Bombylius major*)
Common Wasp (*Vespula vulgaris*)
Hornet (*Vespa crabro*)
Mason Wasp (*Ancistrocerus* sp.)
White-tailed Bumblebee (*Bombus lucorum*)
Honey Bee (*Apis mellifera*)

Red Mason Bees (*Osmia rufa*)
Leaf-cutter bee (*Megachile* sp.)
Turnip Sawfly (*Athalia rosae*).
Common Earwig (*Forficula auricularia*)
Hawthorn Shield Bug (*Acanthosoma haemorrhoidale*)
Greenfly (Family Aphididae)
Squash Bug (*Coreus marginatus*)
Pond Skater (*Gerris lacustris*)
Common Scorpion Fly (*Panorpa communis*)
Snipe-fly (*Rhagio* sp.)

Spiders and Harvestmen

European Garden Spider (*Araneus diadematus*).
Wolf Spider (*Pardosa amentata*)

Two orb web spiders (probably *Metellina* sp.)
An unidentified spider
Harvestman (*Leiobunum rotundum*)

Frogs, snakes, slugs and snails

Common Frog (*Rana temporaria*)
Grass Snake (*Natrix natrix*)
Field Slug (*Deroceras reticulatum*)
A yellow slug (possibly *Deroceras agreste*)
Brown-lipped Snail (*Cepea nemoralis*)
White-lipped Snail (*Cepea hortensis*)
Common Garden Snail (*Helix aspersa*)
Amber Snail (*Succinea putris*)

Other natural history titles by Brambleby Books

Bird Words
Hugh D. Loxdale
ISBN 9780954334734

British and Irish Butterflies
Adrian M. Riley
ISBN 9780955392801

The Wild Flowers of the Isle of Purbeck
Edward Pratt
ISBN 9780955392849

Arrivals and Rivals
2nd Edition
Adrian M. Riley
ISBN 9780954334796

UK500: Birding in the fast lane
James Hanlon
ISBN 9780954334789

Feathers and Eggshells
Natalie Lawrence
ISBN 9780954334772

www.bramblebybooks.co.uk